Pine

Books by Jonathan Johnson

Poetry

Mastodon, 80% Complete

In the Land We Imagined Ourselves

May Is an Island

Pine

Memoir

Hannah and the Mountain: Notes Toward a Wilderness Fatherhood

The Desk on the Sea

Fiction

The Little Lights of Town

Pine

Jonathan Johnson

Carnegie Mellon University Press
Pittsburgh 2025

Acknowledgments

Thank you to the editors of the following publications in which these poems, sometimes in slightly different form, first appeared:

Appalachian Places: "Ancestry on Glenelg Bay" and "Glenelg Wedding Eve"
The Arkansas International: "Amy"
The Glacier: "Route"
Redactions: *"I just can't remember who to send it to,"* "My Brilliant Former Student and Friend Twenty Years Younger than Me and Struggling to Find a Meaningful Job Ended His Life in November," and "Reading Seferis at Sea"
Terrain.org: "Hometown for the Summer," "In a New Grief," and "When Something's Good, Keep It."

"Samu as Cutting Wood a Winter Ahead" and "Twenty-Five Miles from Milk" appeared in the anthology, *Yooper Poetry: On Experiencing Michigan's Upper Peninsula* (Modern History Press).

Book design by Connie Amoroso

Library of Congress Control Number 2025931894
ISBN 978-0-88748-715-6

Printed and bound in the United States of America

10 9 8 7 6 5 4 3 2 1

for Cody Smith

Contents

Prologue

Marquette

Glenelg and Grace in Distant Ruins

Prologue

In a New Grief

The world heals in around a house.
Look at the old photos.
            Black and white,
bare. No sycamore shade.
            No rose bushes
up to the porch rail. The first owners
are new to the new wood, recently
            forest and not yet settled.
All the floors perfectly level.
            The first layer of paint.
The first generation of starlings only now
            building nests in the eve.

Marquette

Chorus of the Cold Weather Body Farm

Children picking up our bones
Will never know that these were once
As quick as foxes on the hill
—Wallace Stevens

If not for a beauty strip of maples and pines
and the wire-crowned fence,
screened forest green
for our privacy, our high acre
would sit exposed on the ridge. Like a porch
overlooking the highway and Lake Superior horizon.

We chose this. Air open
to the sky. Insects diligent
as a shipyard salvage crew.
Little animal snouts following hunger
to find and touch us
with their acquisitive wetness. Crows.

Surprisingly, there isn't much smell,
assures the Anthropology Department Head.
You have to be literally inside the facility
and have fresh donations.
The tinnitus singing of overhead powerlines
accompanies our silent recitation.

Forever donors, we'll leave nothing to scatter
to summer waves. When our work
in this field is done, our curated bones
will wait in their cases to teach
hushed sophomores the genders and heights,
ancestries and accidents we once called ourselves.

Meanwhile, we gather here like professors.
Virtuous field far beyond
form and emptiness recite
the farmhouse-temple disciples of Zen across town.
Deep in the dorms, students of human taphonomy
sleep late with young hands and fresh sheets.

We pretend to be victims
to the sunrise. We soften
into our cushions of soil.
Like our neighbors in the stone castle
state prison behind us who eat from trays
on steel under electric light,

we'll winter here beside the lake's
white desert of ice. *No color,*
no sound, no smell, no taste, no touch;
no object of mind. . . . We do not ask you
driving by below to consider us.
Hold your wheel warm toward town

through spindrift snaking
white across blacktop. Cold is the point
of this place, how we freeze and desiccate,
our mouths' mummification in wind,
until, for a time, the snow's solemn accumulation
inters us after all.

"What's Your Name, and What City Are You Calling From?"

Whatever it is that's wrong with me
is softened by the snow piled parking-meter high
between me and the sidewalk in my little downtown,
the perpetual flow of gold marquee bulbs
and the neon letters lighting red, one by one,
D-E-L-F-T at the old theatre,
stoplights agreeing on green, the bundled woman
climbing the post office steps, package
in her gloved hands, the long, melt-wet essss
of each car passing mine where
I idle in the year's end outside Babycakes
waiting for my wife and daughter to see if they have
any chocolate chip muffins left and listen
to Sam from Skandia call an Instant Request
into Q107's Q Line from the backside of Palmer
for Billy Idol because, he says, "The sun's on the snow
and I'm on the road and just wanna rebel yell, Jim!"
I search my memory for Sams from high school.
None. But the same sun twinkles the tinsel
dangling from the DIGS pub awning.
I used to work night and day, Norman Rockwell wrote,
possessed by a sort of panic that I'd lose everything
if I didn't drive myself. It was his psychologist
who coined *identity crisis* down the block
as the hypochondriac painted his Stockbridge
in a main street studio above Alice's Restaurant
at which Arlo Guthrie reminds us we can get
anything we want, which seems about right,
when my wife and daughter emerge and all
through Sam's requested *more! more! more!*

I have thought nothing about my mother's blood
on the scrubs of the breathless doctor who laughed
about having run up four flights of stairs to get there
or the deaths sooner or (God, please, God)
later awaiting every remaining one of us
and they have a white bag of chocolate chip muffins.

I just can't remember who to send it to.

More and more the world
in which I live no longer exists.
Mother. Grandfather. Now friends.
Addresses. The faculty now
aren't replacements, just the faculty.
As for lost romances, mine
have joined the vast anonymous.
Every weather is the weather
of loss. Poets who lived as I
would live become mere books.
My marginalia unread by even me.
I am loved out here. Yes.
But it's a strange land.
Where the songs of home
sound achingly the same.

The Snowplows of My Hometown

The snowplows of my hometown
now flash green beacons
in addition to the old amber.
I cannot stress enough
the significance of this development.
Also, now the roof light strobes
instead of spins. This will require
a whole new mythology. Something
perhaps to do with aircraft
signaling starboard through a blizzard.
Maybe the pulse of a pulsar,
collapsed star come down to us
in the adopted emerald of luck,
calling by the darkened houses
of its circuit, freeing the people
of Spruce Street past Arch, Michigan,
Ohio, Hewitt, Prospect, Crescent,
little Albert, Park, to turn
on its path up the Christmas-
light constellations of Magnetic.
It was there the town's old poet
would sit up late at the head
of a long captain's table and write
and wait for the old, amber
lighthouse beam to sweep into sight
a thousand ghost snowflakes
before the rumble of the blade
pushed past its curling,
spindrifting wave and the amber
flash crossed the wall to cross
and light his face like a greeting.

The Muse guiding him home again.
Or a siren he managed once more
to outlast and pass, her one note
spinning dimmer, dimmer, dimmer. . . .
Or once, across town, drifted in
against Friday night movie plans
and my friends, when my dad said,
"I don't think you're gonna get out,"
that sweeping, yellow searchlight came
leading Brian Guenther's Suburban.
That is, his parents' Suburban.
The one they used to plow the lot
of their grocery on Washington.
Only now ferrying eight juniors,
blade down, through a moiling sea
of snow, so I could say, "Bye dad!"
So this is aging. Knowing here,
or in some other northern town,
a young poet walks through the snow
from a kiss, or wanting a kiss,
and hears the snow-muffled growl
and sees in that new green winking
the approach of a companion
and nods as they pass, each into
someday's old mythology.

Winter Shore

You can almost see your erasure here
in snow-mottled sand and scalded grass.
In the wavelets' pulse you can almost hear
the companion you make of loneliness.
It's almost a pocket stone, the sky this low.
A few old houses on the ridge play dead
for the empty playground's almost sorrow.
Alone, you can say the thing you almost said
years ago at her door a few blocks inland
where others keep the empty flowerpots.
The lighthouse bricks and ice-caked rock islands
smolder inside with former suns, almost, but not
really. The horizon snows. And love as it was
is nowhere near this gray cove as it is.

Over the Bridge at the Mouth of the Dead

Gather in, my ghosts. I've scoured the town for you.
The old power plant's mastodon buildings, abandoned
bare trees on the bank between river and frozen pond.

Winter gray turnouts along the shore. Slow past former houses.

Old cemetery in the snow, obviously. Empty picnic pavilion,
cold-to-the-touch table view to islands and low mountains,
a time before sorrow. Lighthouse on the shipless horizon.

Then today came an approaching constellation, young family
in coats and gloves and hats, all five with bright headlamps
though it was only fading afternoon. Only a park.

The bouncing, wandering stars eclipsed their faces.

The father gathered snow from a bench, pitched the snowball
deliberately short of one of his little ones, a provocation answered
with a toss from a big, pink glove at the end of a short, bundled arm.

Tell me it's not so bad, being replaced. Tell me
it's like watching others searchlight
their wintry way down shore and into the woods.

Maybe I'm Not Grieving Right

A heresy
to say, I know. But when I show my friend's widow
the photo I found of the two of them
and she says it'll be five years for a moment
I think she means some other anniversary
and say the stock *No* and mean it.

Yesterday's snow makes scale-model mountain ranges
between sidewalk and curb. Avalanche chutes
and scree fields of icy sand, ridgeline of summits
unsummited. Routes the eye traces
from inside the Third Street Bagel Shop window.

Five years is a whiteout confusion.
Thin air altitude pulling the chest outward. Steady.
Down the block from his house (his former house?)
waves will be rolling onto frozen sand.

The picture is taken from across their table,
whitefish and baked potatoes, a glass of milk,
still life over which my friend and his wife smile,
leaning together, their heads touching. My friend's smile
has an element of surprise. Hey, here we all are!
As my wife and I saw them from our side.

Really, I really cannot just walk down there
and step unknocking inside and call his name.
The endless neighborhood to which that name
was attached has emptied of every citizen,
and under the bare trees I wander.

Genesis

The lake looked much like this a thousand years ago.
Moonlight on snowed-over ice all the way across
to snow in the dark pines. Stars.
Except for the red pulse at the top of a new radio tower.

Nagasaki, Marquette

Let's hope it's a good one
—Lennon and Ono

The erasure I can imagine, sudden
nothingness, children as if they never were.
Or, if not imagine, at least conceive.
There then not. With no other harm or fear.
The plane tiny by then on the horizon.
Incinerations, partial and complete.
What we do not want to hear is Mama,
English word already widespread before the war.
Mama, they called, blind and burned. *Mama.*
(Find me.) Beyond that—agonies of hours,
of days (what were days?), of weeks, months—
understanding fails. Or is it surrenders?

So that now my small, lakeside city wakes,
gray with snowfall through last night's Christmas lights.
So this is history. So we're taught. No bomb,
no grandfather-in-law's homecoming. No bomb,
no wife. No wife—. And here's the erasure
I can't conceive. Would trade anything against.
Child, child, child. My precious child.
But no one asks. And that's not fallout
falling on our roofs and filling our yards.
Those aren't embers, twinkling in our windows
and trees, spilling molten from our eves.

The world's made new with one birth, but where
are the harms of someone long before us?
O come let us adore Him. Her. All of them.
O holy night. The stars are brightly shining.

O. O. O. Shape the mouth makes in soft reverence.
Oh, it's not the screams I can't conjure—
my daughter's ear ache that ER Christmas Eve—
it's what's inside the scream empathy abandons
at the makeshift hospital primary school
just beyond the incineration zone.
Little desks pushed together for tables.

Have those snow-muffled morning bells forgotten?
It's not the Child that made the world new.
It was the suffering. And so we went home
with our own little person, her pain relieved,
asleep already, at last, on the drive
and all night to wake and descend the stairs
to see among her gifts the Seven Dwarfs
she adored, standing a couple inches small
in line, atop one of the wrapped boxes.
She froze and cried, *Mama,* fear in her voice
at the joy of having what she wanted.
Fear at having what she wanted known.

Hometown for the Summer

The houses in the old neighborhood
are faces. Some dignified.
Kept optimistically up.
Some crumble, exposing more
of what they're made of.
Letting in more weather.
Most are like us.
You have to want to look
a moment longer. Then worth it.
In rows, they watch us pass, their children.
Humming. Weeping. So much desire.
Until we leave. Until we die.
They do not wait for our return.
Patient parents, they do not call us in
until almost dark.

Matins

Shield the joyous
—Book of Common Prayer

Amy's upstairs in the only shower
so Chad went for a quick splash down at the cove
last night Anya checked in from New York with friends
I've got the smoked whitefish omelets warming on low
while Simon and Garfunkel sing *lie la lie*
according to Jim of Jim and Ray at the pub
Kurt's back from Guatemala painting a few months
on a house on the ridge overlooking the harbor
where I'll go look for him later
and Russ must be to the library by now for the grand piano
he'll be expecting me at the coffee shop
with the day's poem this afternoon
thirty-two years and he's still not done
with me taking everyone and everything's mortality so seriously
even as George Harrison now wouldn't have a clue
if not for someone and forty-five minutes of Zen
at the temple and five miles run around the island
and bare feet on these warm porch floorboards
have me at ease as since I don't know when
a moment to offer if I could send it back in time
to any one of my numberless exiles of dread
until Jerry Garcia just has to chime in (damn it)
and remind me that when life looks like easy street
there is danger at your door which brings that old
cold familiar tightening across the chest
I'll try to loosen with a few slow breaths into the breeze

Common

Seagulls are a good test of one's
    current state of awareness.
Where they are, they are everywhere,
    wheeling in the high air,
finding and following a current
    with little adjustments.
"Trash birds," you hear. "Like rats"
    (who might also make
a good measure of your capacities
    for wonder). "Rats with wings."
Okay, yes. They can be about that
    white when the sky clears.
We eat and strew our garbage too.
    We are nothing like rare.
And our spirits imagine their own wings
    translucent, sailing in the sun.

Twenty-Five Miles from Milk

The piano in the pickup doesn't know
it's leaving loon song over dusk water,
the heron's glide, the duck's bank, and dragonfly.
The woman's childhood feet on warm dock planks.
Her parents' rare afternoon in the loft
alone, making her. The drowsy specks of flame
that rose into the stars, the moon, the Mars.
There's no indignity in the careful climb,
slow up the rutted drive cathedraled in pine.
The totter, jostle, and jolt at the switchback,
the grip and gravel spit where it's always the worst,
where once, in snow, the dad broke an axel
gunning for the top, story of cables and a come-along.
I'll show you the turtles! but the piano
will play its rubato in town without the water-
wing-flap of a rising goose. Under stars
with silhouettes of pine, the log walls have long settled.
Twenty-five years the sawdust's gone from their hair.
The grandfather hasn't the heart to tell the trees
the new owner's rich and mean. Breathing alone
in town the town's changes, awaiting a tune, the piano
has no lyric for loving just one piece of land.

The Trees of Town

Here, we say. Not here.
Okay, they agree and root
beneath our portioned sod and sidewalks
and branch between our powerlines
and over our gabled lives.
Their patience is beyond understanding,
for which they become the low sky.
Undulating like anemones
they show invisible currents of breeze.
They receive their birds and release them effortlessly.
In summer there is no winter.
Their every unscrolled leaf maps its own eternity,
vessels to carry the sun's freight home.
We are fools, mostly, going about
our worried and determined designs
beneath them. Then we look up
and see they have been waiting.

Two Neighborhood Robins

The female stood in the street under arches of elm
and did not fly or even flinch at our walking past.

Later, from the porch, we saw her again,
at the end of our driveway now. Still, when people startled
and stepped around her. Injured. Or maybe sick.
Indifferent to the crumbs we gently tossed.

By evening, she'd crossed the quiet, narrow lane.
For shade? Cover of a parked car's back bumper?

When the frantic chirping startled me from my book
and I looked to glimpse her carried up in the raven's talons,
the male chasing after, I should not have called you
out to stand on the lawn beside me and shade our eyes

and see her squirming in that dark grip on the neighbor's chimney cap.
Him whirling just above, helpless, as one of us one day will be.

Tensile

Of what must be seven or eight segments
that constitute the web in the corner of the window
only one wedge shows, sun-silvered and trembling
like the wires of a zither. Someone's work. Waiting
in the morning. Like the offshore fishnet set yesterday
and undulating with the minor currents while the boat's
tied in the harbor. This is the town's third summer
without my friend. I will not see him on the sidewalk
and smiling to recognize me in the cool, early sun,
as a breeze moves over my skin.

The Historic House Painter

He rides the rigging high over Spruce Street,
the closer sun and clouds to catch his hair.
He scrapes thin layers from the sky to flakes
that fall and flurry blue as days away.
When children oar below on bikes, he waits,
a little god to clear their air. To love
and pass unseen, the clean new grain of years
affixed to the mast, his fingers, and face.
A harbor somewhere. Someone's gable window
from which she looks up from his page from time
to time so not to miss his horizon's
arrival. He opens his blue sail shake
by shake shimmering dry in the wind.
Far above, turning seagulls signal land.

Samu as Cutting Wood a Winter Ahead

—early autumn, Alger County

After the rain I promise myself just
one tank before a late dinner.

Sharpened chain sinks through lichen
and gray skin to open a cascade

of maple's hidden interior as blond
sawdust. The little poles go quickly.

The thick, dark trunks take a while,
down on one knee in the hot exhaust

and damp fiber smell as the saw bar
disappears. Steady growl and shush

of full throttle through earmuffs.
When the gap finally begins to close

at the top of a log, pull the bar clear
from the bottom. Never touch the ground.

The saw idles back, break locked,
resting on the stack of stove lengths.

A spider climbs from a deep bark fissure,
runs, and I remember this morning's zendo

vow to save all beings and lift this one's terrain
and set it down on the stack carefully.

Later, nearing the end of this log deck,
I start to wonder, each time

the throttle hesitates, if this is it—empty.
Then the engine growls and grabs again.

So it goes, not yet old but getting older.
Inside, someone I love is seasoning the steelhead.

I move faster. Cuts up. Cuts down.
Toss the lengths to either side,

cut again. Revving through rings
of all those standing seasons that made this tree,

I remember. Joy burns not by time or effort.
Virtuous field far beyond form and emptiness.

And with a few logs left, a faltering,
a surrender in the trigger. A sigh.

I pull my earmuffs off. The engine ticks.
Dusk. Into which an eagle somewhere

whistles a note, softer than one would expect,
above the house, the still water, the woods.

When Something's Good, Keep It

The night-clouds rained and took all morning moving on,
so that now, afternoon opens its bright prism
on everything—cool breeze through the anemones of trees,
skin of a passing woman's shoulder, gleaming chrome fender
of her bike, black iron, and translucent streetlamp glass.
Like the granite-gray, six-foot, resolute-browed
Easter Island head between pots of blue asters on a stoop
and supervising the corner of Third and Ridge,
I have taken myself most seriously.
Fears and desires. Desires and fears.
Meanwhile, this clear, easy joy had been waiting for me.
That passing red Jeep guy has stacked his roof high
with equipage. Out he goes!
We are born clean of clothes, money, or name,
numberless moments lined up to receive us.

Glenelg and Grace in Distant Ruins

The Still Voice Ruin

All the dials in the unpolished brass are down.

The end goes on, a borderline of wind outside this broken down,
antique manor machine.

What was, the birds turned dust do not sing through the dark.

Were there prayers? Yes, vast and empty now as night ragged
landscape.

What the glass lets in. What the glass refuses.

Nothing. Free. Nothing. Free. Nothing. And free. And free.
And free. And no thing.

The candles. Out. Listening.

Return

Beyond and below an iron gunnel
the constant foam of ferry wake
rolls over black, afternoon sea
off Skye. A patch of sun
silvers the sound halfway to Rùm.

So is this too my life?
So whose life is this? Old book

Where mainland begins again
greylag geese lift leaving the kale
and call sharply into an arrow
over elms along the headstone meadow
of my orphan mother's childhood name.

shelved deep in the stacks while I
was extremely elsewhere.

This is the recovery she taught me.
The world's indifference makes a companion
if you ask. Through a former roof abandoned
by a new lord to weather against
the family's return, a rowan grows.

In the unseen entries and exits
of centuries, I am a generation.

The tree's narrow protection comes late
to its cottage on grief's vast estate,
so I claim some myself. This garden fence,
an evening's birthright. To sit
on toppled stones her grandparents stacked.

The Glen

I've walked five fields of road
to the coffee cup I forgot at the gate
this morning, a gift from America
I sent cousin Megan the Christmas
after she and Jon came across
to celebrate their first anniversary.

The little artifact declares its far origin
The Mason Jar, Cheney, Washington
in blue on white enamel from the grass
atop a moss-mottled stone wall.
How *un*like dominion to the indifferent
bracken hills that vault away to granite.

When Usiden, eighty-eight now, pulls up
and rolls down his window for a chat,
why does it thoroughly delight me
his first words are *You've been working*
as he nods to my trousers, smeared
with the ground of Jon and Meg's garden?

For all the relations' names we share
in the kirkyard, so many faded to nothing,
I want to tell him I'm grateful our lives
overlap a while—His boyhood Gaelic
he'll gladly translate. *Fraoch,* heather.
Bothan, shepherd's cottage. *Muir,* the sea.

My bewildered longing that leads me.
The steep, one-lane road in over
Ratagan, my storyline. So I've decided—

And so this old crofter seems to agree
when his gnarled hand reaches through
the truck window to welcome me back.

Ancestry on Glenelg Bay

The gate to this kirkyard beside the sea
remains unlocked. Swings rusty. Most of the stones
stand as no more than stones again, blessings,
dates, and names gone to lichen, rain, and wind.
No one comes for anyone here anymore.
The last of their visitors has long gone
to the new cemetery north of the Glen More.
There, brides still lay bouquets on grans' firm lawns,
and already the elms have grown broad shade
inland from open gales. There, smooth granite
enunciates each of the erasures delayed
in sharp-etched dates and prayers enameled white.
While here, with steps the sea-wet sod inters,
one remembers not who but that they were.

Realism

Amy and I walked down from the farmhouse
to the village, stopping to step through the cemetery gate
for a moment with my mother's family name again
and again in granite under the big oak.

Sun crossed the opposite pasture and climbed
the wooded side of the glen. The granite remained.

We walked on to the shop for a birthday card
and chocolate roses, then cut across on the path
through sheep beside the sea to Riverfoot cottage.
Christina opened the door in her kitchen apron.

Will you come in? No, we were just stopping
with our birthday wishes. *I won't tell you
how old I am.* A quiet amazement herself.
Eighty-six. Congratulations, we said.

I won't be long. She glanced skyward.
But I'll take each day as it comes.

Glenelg Wedding Eve

Seaward, night's tide has risen already
over the island's mountains into mist
that comes down from and over everything
through which smoke and music ascend.
A chorus of laughter. The Sound of Sleat
blackens early into late-October evening
out the inn's fogged windows. From Skye's
unpeopled slopes two miles offshore,
this village must be a wee constellation
of close, amber stars. Between darknesses,
this fireside chair deepens warm and a guitar
blurs faster, faster to lift the voices climbing
the spin behind. . . .
                                        Inland, upriver to the wild
top of the glen, far above the last light,
there's no lock on the only door. No one within.
Bricks of peat stacked beside the silent hearth
even now, always. That shepherdless cottage
teaches patience for patience. The nature of love
from its cool, unseen, and ancient stone.

—for Cousin Megan
and (tomorrow) Cousin Jonathan

Among Ancestors' Wild Summits

In a late slant of sun
I hike high from the lone
shepherd's cottage
and look back from the slope
as though on my life
so small from this far

After November, December

His choice to be dead
keeps coming true   suddenly
for me   come great joys   thunder
rain   a Greek island winter
in an old house   his
quiet smile   here   in both sounds

My Brilliant Former Student and Friend Twenty Years Younger than Me and Struggling to Find a Meaningful Job Ended His Life in November

Beside a taverna stove fire
on an ancient Aegean harbor,
winter rain and rocking sailboats,
the ancient spruce in Yellowstone
comes to me. Twenty years
I visited it, on the ridge
over which the tiny lake
finally appears, summit cathedraled.
The trunk massive. Cracked orange.
Broken off and dead but
for one high branch,
green flag stiff in the wind,
until last June that too
had fallen, needles dry brown,
and I saw all was lost, ruins
tumbled from the spire, wild
roses' fragrant tide rising
around an abandoned lighthouse.

Defenseless

I find myself alone at the bow
of a fishing boat much older than me.
Worn wood hull. Rust.
Crusted paint and resin. Sea-bleached
equipage. Anchored in cool winter sun
and breeze. Greece is an island horizon
of baked rock and shrubs.
Turkey, distant mountains' snow
the color of a few clouds.
If you shutter your eyes,
the sun warms your face. An old trick.
The smells of brine and winch grease.
Slosh of small waves. Don't tell me
a life can't learn to love you again.

Reading Seferis at Sea

Forgotten on the shore the sea's secrets
"Love's Discourse"

But also, forgotten on the sea
the shore's secrets. Or if not
forgotten, small. Scaled down.
Like the hills of Rhodes
on the barren side from
low against the gunwale
of the old fishing boat
on small waves. Or sandstone
buildings of Marquette, child's
model of a town from
out in the dusk harbor
where I row my dory. From
not as far out as you'd think,
the names I carry
dim like worn coins.

Somewhere on the Ruins of Somewhere Else

In a very Land Roverish Athenian suburb
I've never been before and don't expect
to be again, the smell of cigarette smoke
at the outdoor café smells of sweet childhood.
Before they quit. Mom and Dad. Home,
our little student family housing apartment,
when a friend would call and the cord
reached the kitchen table where she'd sit
and crack a can of Tab and put her feet up
and laugh and tap ashes in an ash tray.
Or her basement carrel TA office
in the summer when she had the Selectric
to herself to type hours about Wordsworth.
Where we'd find her, Dad, my sister,
and me, and they'd swap, and we'd leave him
to light a Now in *his* TA office, some desks
in an old classroom, a wall of high windows
and tall blinds through which sunlight made
pages of afternoon above him at his novel,
and she took us to play in the campus fountain,
water running over stone blocks on which
my sister and I would climb while she watched,
alive, and smiled from the stone bench beside.

—for Ann

You Travel Awhile

You travel awhile with some people,
sing together to the turning wheels and wild hills,
and soon feel as if you'll always know them.
Later, in a far town alone, you sit at a table
in the sun and can think of only two names.
And soon those will be gone. There is no
moral failure. This must be how it is for the earth.
The rocky cove beaches curve around exactly us.
The melt river parts cold around our specific shins.
Sunshine warms the metal table and lined paper
the same as the skin on this writing hand.
In its infinite ways, the earth knows each of us
it travels with. Sincere friends it soon forgets.

When I Think of Cathedrals

It’s calculable, I suppose, how many lifetimes
of living went into this. Spreading wet mortar
and setting the next stone with a wiggle.
A handsaw through boards to build scaffolding.
Hands gripping that wood to climb.
Someone’s butt on the planks. Feet dangling.
Thick feel of fingers curled around a handle.
Welcome cool air of a cloud shading the sun.
Leaning in to look up close. To check.
Squeak of the pully. Sharp fibers of rope.
Someone rose early and made bread to send.
Sometimes she walked to bring bread here.
To say hello, when his day’s work was still low.
There would be generations of work right here.
Elsewhere in a workshop, the smooth muscle of marble.
Smell of smoking coals and heat of a lead bead
poured down the grove between blue and green glass.
Someone sat at a broad table working a complex equation.
Parabolas meeting in a pointed arch. Down rib vaults.
Clear span weight, lateral pressure, and counterforces
of flying buttresses. Every tile placed on the pinnacle
where nobody will see. *God will see.* God and the angels
looking down like this, everyone so small below.
There are seconds in every oak shaving fallen
from a timber’s tenon. Thunk of mallet closing the joint.
Should we count the time someone way up
spent watching a pigeon sail down, green sheen of feathers,
to land on the windlass beam beside him?
A bishop’s ride over cobble bumps toward the Vatican
to lobby for this construction? A weaver’s hours
over the blanket that grew old to end up folded on the floor

under someone's knees as he widened the nave mosaic?
I don't think of God. Not directly anyway. Grace ascends
the columns toward the infinite azure of human attention.
I also think of all the time since, when my own shoe wears
however many more molecules from the deep concavity
in a stone tread up the spiral stairs toward gargoyles.
The bells. Bones long out of their long-gone flesh
down in the crypt someone else dug with a shovel.
The iron handrail worn just a little smoother, a little shinier,
by the warm palm of a kid on a field trip, stopped
to stare at the intricate shield carved on the sarcophagus lid.
Meanwhile, a thousand years ago a ruin reverses itself
up from stacks of stone on the ground around it
as another child looks out a gable window over rooftops
and trails of chimney smoke to where her father goes
each morning while she's still sleeping.

Fade

For a guy who was broke half the time,
Junkets, friends called him and let's call him ours,
had a genius for real estate. Hampstead?
A block off the heath? Come on.
And the Spanish Steps? I mean, *right on*
the Spanish Steps, second floor, overlooking the fountain.
They were rentals, of course. Always a roommate.
But if he'd set out to predict his pilgrimage museums
(he didn't), he could not have done better.
He certainly bested the six-foot blue-blood Byron's abbey,
which would have pleased him no end.
Twenty years old, I came to 26 Piazza de Spagnia and wrote
my first published poem overlooking the fountain
from his last window. Later I paid a street artist
fifty thousand lire to sketch the house, looking up
at the open shutters. Thirty-six years
that sketch has been fading, to near nothingness now.
Like words on the mug in my coffee shop back home.
A barista there made it for me, Keats quotes
in ceramic marker everywhere on the white vessel.
Even the handle. All faded away in a year or two.
As though with a wink from the poet whose instructions
for his gravestone consisted of no name
and *Here lies one whose name was writ in water.*
Nobody reads the poem I wrote in 1988 anymore,
though it must be in a campus library or two.
Keats' poems are in tired-spine textbooks
in rows on classroom bookshelves the world over.
Which makes him no less dead.
No less gone from the world, hoping for spring flowers,
like these, a stroll in the sun, like this,

back in Rome thirty-six years later. My own life
a little faded. Some who loved and remembered me
gone. But here I am, on a shaded park bench with my wife,
who asks, "Aim or Amos, Mac used to call me?"
surprised and sad to have forgotten some of a friend already.
She and I, nineteen and twenty, came from the house
out to the cemetery—back then we had to ring the bell
at the gate—where the countryside began
when Keats asked Severn to go see it for him,
and Severn reported back the rural tranquility.
Maybe sheep. Maybe flowers. Where they are both
buried, Severn's infant son's little headstone
between and a bit behind theirs. How's that
for engendering affection? Sixteen years after
Keats' death, his deathbed friend buries his son
beside him. Fifty-eight years later, Severn goes
there too. Another prime location, shade and grass,
a quiet corner. A couple benches. So we go.
So we all go. Poems or no. The days. The days.
All one. His love's letters from Hampstead
down there with him, unopened—he couldn't bear
to read—on his chest, now nothing with that chest.
So how about we give our friend an unseasonably
warm afternoon? A little rally in health.
A stroll up the steps. Up to the hillside
overlooking the pond—like the heath back home,
where he kissed her—let's give him easy breaths,
a while yet to sit on the grass under trees and sky.
Somewhere good to be awhile. What any of us asks.

Wanting It to Count for More

While I was sitting and staring like an asshole
at the grave of John Keats, my student,
my kind, gentle graduate student and friend
and fellow living poet was taking her own life.
Or maybe it was hours earlier, when I was
the American Professor making a few poetry pilgrims
and the museum worker tear up with lesser-known
Keats anecdotes and his wisdom for living
at the house where he died. My kind, gentle student
would not have wanted me to think of myself,
sitting in the cemetery, watching a tall fringe of grass
bend in the breeze and mottled shade before
Here lies one whose name was writ on water
as an asshole. Or, more precisely, a failure
as her teacher and friend. It's fun, giving the young
some of *our* friend (and I call him our friend)
Keats' mortal awareness and urgent beauty.
His of the heart's affections.
His vale of soul making. It feels important,
telling them, each time new, his story, that they too
can be capable of being in uncertainties,
mysteries, doubts, without any reaching
after fact or reason. Among the most useful
words I know. I leave out "irritable"
before "reaching" as freighted differently now.
And I add an example. The big mystery?
How two so opposing conditions of spirit,
how grief—nursing your younger brother to death,
the latest of many—and falling in love with the girl
literally next door, under the same roof, every day
and every *night*, just on the other side of the wall
(and here I slap the board in front of class

JUST on the OTHer SIDE of the WALL),
how hollow sorrow and brimming desire can coexist
in one soul. What are we to *do*? What *are* we to do?
You don't have to solve such contradictions,
Keats is telling us, I tell them. Your life isn't
math. Your life isn't solvable. It's enough just to live it.
I'm speaking to myself, of course. As I was
with the Keats House pilgrims. As I was
to the stone and the grass when I asked to be,
among other things (son, brother, poet,
husband, and father), a worthy teacher and friend.
My student died in her bed with her books
and her own thesis poems. The room
in which Keats died is narrow and tall. On the ceiling—
experts dug to get to the original—are painted flowers.
As if, he remarked, he were already beneath
their blossoms. His friend would open the shutters
to let in the sky. The fountain below gurgled away.
Have you ever seen anyone die, Severn? Keats asked
and said, *I shall die easy. Don't be frightened, be firm.*
And when it was close, and Severn sat exhausted
in the night beside him and worried he would fall asleep
and the candle would go out and Keats wake
frightened in the dark, Severn dipped a thick thread
in the wax and tied it from the bottom of the lit
candle to the wick on the candle beside,
so the flame would rise, one to the other,
and keep the light for his friend.   And my student. . . .
All these stories she adored, the wisdom,
the poems to give us our lives to live as poets. . . .
My student. . . .
                    Her name was Grace and she died alone.

Sally Mann

"Emmett, Jessie and Virginia, 1989"

Remember when our skin held everything—
or what then seemed everything—river sand
and blood, snot, strawberry ice cream,
mud dried to dirt-cracking creases of your hands?
It's not that the world was ours. We were
the world's. Paint, sun, leaves, others' warm skin,
smear and silk of grass found us at the blurred
edge of ourselves. Kiss, scab, fist on the chin.
Remember touch without time or knowing
our perfection or naming it our soul
or knowing we would end, apart, in clothes?
We'd have never thought to call ourselves whole.
Our bodies weren't bodies. They were summer and feral.
We'd not yet begun to abandon the world.

The Last Pregnancy Test

The little girl's hair curls halfway to her boots planted
just behind the teeth from which the escalator cascades.
She refused the hand, dad or maybe grandpa,
and now the man reaches up, calls *Step on honey!*
descending. She half-steps back as I begin
to work the problem from twenty feet of polished
concrete floor behind her, the distance my wife
is already crossing. My wife knows to ask
the sinking man's permission so the child hears.
Knows to ask the child. To offer her hand
and wait. Whatever her voice says as they ride
down together is bright as the silver bulbs high
on the four-story Christmas tree beside them.

Later, our daughter texts a picture of garland
wrapping her campus lamppost. Through the glass
I watch my wife spill food into the porch cat's bowl
and slide her hand firm and slow down the silk
of his muscular spine. I set the phone back
on the counter and feel again the warm stream
of water over my hands rinsing a breakfast plate.
Stream of water I leave falling when she calls me
frantic outside *Hurry! Bring a dishtowel!*

It takes a moment to process how light
the hawk rests in my hands. How insubstantial and still
with the towel over her head. We think we know
the weight of living things. We expect a struggle to live.
She's small for a hawk. The netting tangled and tightened
around her thin talons while she hung and flapped
—for how long?—before my wife saw her. The garden cat

pacing below. When I netted the grapevine in spring
against grazing deer, protection for summer's little grapes
from the blackbirds' adoration, I thought nothing
of further causation. Early winter's hunting hawk,
the vole or finch below. The speed into confusion,
the struggle, this blank desertion of sight.

My wife is fast and precise with the scissors. The bound,
black talons, collapsed in their black wrapping,
neither grip nor struggle against her. Mesh falls aside
as she snips more fibers down a slim, leather leg
to the small, dull claws. I carry the limp hawk
across the garden and set her on a stone. I lift the towel
and expect a slow sorrow. I expect quiet acceptance.
Life's like that. So when she flips and lifts into the air
and flies straight between the pines away
I'm surprised again, by all this woman beside me
can right and free, small on the cold horizon from us.

Art

Torture. The Child Protection Services file
actually used the word. The first time
in my wife's long career as a child therapist
she'd seen that. Months later on the other side
of the world, we're hiking down the cliff path
from the lighthouse when she slips
and the slip becomes a tumble, a roll until
she arrests upside down in bushes I will forever thank.
Scrapes and bruises. Clay mud on her coat
and pants and hands and camera.
Which still works. When she photographs waves
there are only waves. Hours she devotes
to them only, the next one building.
Hours I watch from up shore. When she comes
to me, I mention the fall, my fear, watching her go.
"I'm okay though," she says loud over the surf.
"That was actually awesome! I'm kind of a badass."
When she sleeps that night, the waves through the window
roar and shush. Roar and shush. Roar. And shush.

In Nazaré for the Waves when Some Friends Are Dying and Others Dead

Maybe the point of our contingency
is to feel permanent awhile.
To look through mist-freckled glasses
at our wife and grown daughter
on the beach. The world's biggest waves
rising to walls that fall and fall
as though they need never land.

The Farm, the Cabin, High Wilderness West

Pine

the scent in dry summer sun
cracks the bark outgrowing
the shape insisting itself across landscape
the needles' satiny breeze anemones
crushed cones in dirt road dust
chartreuse lichen living on the dead
lower remnants of limbs
cool mottled shadow across new grass
rising through dead needle thatch
smell years ago of the seasons through saw blade
swirl of grain around riverstone knots in the ceiling
bleached deadfall spine and gray limb bristle
in the sagebrush buttercup and purple grass widows
bare silhouette of a long-standing dead
fossil root reach of an upturned stump
pitch dried to a white crust in the cordwood
amber snap in the night stove winter
their mountain slope plural
a single grasp unfurling above cumulus canopy
mist snagging and slipping free
agate of rain hanging from a needle's end
the pond's perfect inversion deep green
cut open by a mallard's slow crossing
hollow column ruin of black marble
up silver eras after the empire of fire
every night and day cathedraling a small clearing
for black robed crows calling prayers
from high in the ancient architecture
alone in a timothy hayfield with a shed dress of shade
the tower and sapling and straight and tangled
bent wrought vault long lean wind twisted company

up from the earth to start the sky
the canyon they make of a highway
the velvet curtain they edge a meadow
the beginning and end they make of a coast
snow bows hold sagging and shrug
their gentle promise to outlast us

Route

—Cheney to Brewster, Washington

Out of the timber and into wheat-field horizon and
dry-board barns to Davenport comes

a freedom, George Jones "He Stopped Loving Her Today,"
and Elwood the old Crown Vic's new studs

humming the sunwarm November highway, those "letters dated 1962"
until "Blue Eyes Cryin' in the Rain" comes and kills me

again, kills him again, Grandpa, blues blue as this living day.
Good as it is, pulled off at Dean's Drive Inn, cinder blocks

like a summer's stack of hay under new pole-shed roof,
what I want to say's not this road at all, much as Vet's Day flags

flying the two blocks of town's telephone poles
and the two girls off school walking their mukluks

across the gravel parking lot make a kind of company.
What I want to say's tucked back in the forty-years-ago

mountains of Idaho behind me. The farmhouse kitchen.
Cold enamel of that sink at the little window

overlooking the fir-shagged, summit-ridge sunrise over Butler.
Cold of surface-well water from the tap, just enough

for the soap-sudded plastic dishpan because a surface well
can always run dry, though ours never did. His clear emerald

Skin Bracer bottle catching the sun on the sill. Snap of cedar
kindling in the cookstove. Wood grain sheet paneling

holding the nail where my own flannel, hand-me-down shirt
hung, that paneling my uncles put up when a little money

came in when I was too young to remember the walls before,
all the way into the sitting room with the nails

where his guitar hung with Grandma's homemade paintings
of other country scenes. Yellow leaves, waterwheel, a lane.

An empty cattle trailer rattles by and the only thing for all this loss
is more road, Willie's "Angel Flyin' Too Close to the Ground"

speeding after me, willow ditch, and the cop-shock dip and lift
and almost soar of a disused railroad crossing

past a forever-sidetracked wooden boxcar, Northern Pacific,
with a wooden door like the ones he built

way back in mythology to make the down payment.
Eighty acres. The log camp kitchen skidded onto the ridge

and left there for a farmhouse, the barn, alfalfa field up the hay road
through tamarack and fir and cedar thick enough for him

and four sons on crosscuts to make the payments.
I got what I wanted. The cabin in aspen—

the site I picked walking with him when I was twelve,
where he carved *Jon's site 1979*

with his Old Timer pocketknife into the gray-speckled bark
        and the scar rose rough beside the metal roof

I screwed down and the window from which I could watch him
        and Grandma with her walking stick

after the mini strokes, walking from the farmhouse up the two-track
        that led through the woods nowhere else but here. —There.

Here Edna's in Davenport has a huckleberry milkshake and
        good glass on three sides but I drive past.

Marty Robbins' west Texas cowboy is weary but can't stop to rest,
        gets his one final kiss and Felina goodbye

just past the gazebo park across from Napa and Wheatland Bank.
        Uncle Steve cut that window in the cabin wall of tamarack

logs he fell and I skidded behind the Farmall H,
        and when, looking back to check the choker cable's hold

on one of those stringy-bark-slick logs, I high-centered on a stump,
        it was Steve who crawled under with the same chainsaw

he'd used building his house, too, up his own road into the woods
        from Grandma and Grandpa's, and cut away at the stump until

the cracked and sun-faded rubber of that big tractor tire
        settled back plump onto the pine needle mulch forest floor.

Steve's still up there. I'm not, excepting a weekend
        now and then. "Stay on the Farm, Jon." Among the last words

Grandpa ever said to me, reaching up over the chrome rail
to take my hand in the softness of his. "Stay on the Farm."

And "Yes" I said. "Yes." For all those walks we took on his trail.
For my name on the aspen. My flannel shirt on the nail

above the kindling box beside the kitchen woodstove.
That house is gone now. A few years sinking into its hand-dug

cellar and Steve couldn't stand to pass the slow-rising tide
of grass around the wreck so took it all at once with the dozer.

So now, when the tunnel of cottonwoods opens at the end
of the county road and the slow crackle of my tires

climbs the driveway from the mailbox past the rusted flatbed log truck,
there's nothing there on the ridge beside the two huge firs.

"Proceed to the route," Mapquest insists over John Prine
who doesn't remember me or the Farm when he sings

that objects in the mirror may appear closer than reality,
and a hawk stalls and dives into sage

and I am alone. Outliving everything I knew to love
when I was learning how. How it was to sit in the chrome

and vinyl lawn chairs with coffee in the glass mugs and visit.
Visit. Where's that verb gone? Sit and visit.

Who am I supposed to be this far from that? What am I out here
looking for, sentimental about big cars and old country music?

Meanwhile, that copper Beemer's getting impatient behind me,
    so it's off for the broke-down rest stop, a cold seltzer

and a slice of pizza from tinfoil in the cooler. The picnic tables
    have little roofs with weathered shingles that cup

and curl and grow moss and make me think
    of the cedar shakes back before the barn fell in.

It rises so high in my memory, the high hay door
    with its pully hangs open in the sky and gaps in the roof

show moments of that same blue like cloud breaks.
    I'm a fool, I know, but it's hard to go there now,

to stand in deep grass from the seeds of long-gone hay
    by the low, tin roof of the pumphouse

and cut firewood from a logging slash pile beside all that
    empty where the barn should be. No evidence

but the timothy rising a little taller, the green a little thicker there.
    "Proceed to the route," she says brightly.

The idea was to be a cowboy. And he did run a few head of Hereford.
    For a while, anyway. I'd cut the bail twine and spill the hay

from the tailgate of Uncle Richard's turquoise Chevy
    crawling low gear across the frost

in the field out past the outhouse. Ten years
    that truck sat up on blocks behind the machine shed

and me without the money to make it go again and now
it's off the place. Steve saw it once at Lost in the Fifties

(though it's a '65) restored and running again in low
down Cedar in Sandpoint. If only I'd had the money.

If Grandpa'd had the money maybe the barn and house
would still stand. Old Wobbly that he was,

once he bought the place he never again worked
to make someone else money. And there never was much

in crosscut stud logging and a yearling steer or two every spring.
So the cellar stayed dirt, slowly rotting the old skids

under the house, tilting the bedroom floor two two-by-fours under
the headboard feets' worth, and the barn roof thinned like his hair,

and now he'd still be gone from the place even so.
So what else did I expect? Decaf from the Corner Café

in Creston, but not the black and chrome cookstove.
It's a South Bend, not a Monarch like ours,

but much the same otherwise. Only here repurposed
as a side table for silverware and coffee cups.

Maybe Milton got it wrong. Maybe there's no seraph
at the gate with flaming sword. Maybe there's no gate,

and Eden's open but the timber's been thinned out, brush piles
left to molder, the old bower an abandoned homestead.

Knapweed, vetch, and sapling pines taking back the pasture
for Chaos. The easy company of angels over.

God simply gone. Maybe *that's* the Fall, not distance.
Making exiles of us all and leaving our maker's name

on the mailbox. Which is also ours—the name and
address, always to remind us of the loss.

How, for example, did Donald Hall stand it, going back to Eagle Pond?
The grandparent summers right there and nowhere.

Privilege, the new poets would rightly say. Poor, white,
twentieth century, ivy guy faced his loss

did he? Okay, fair point. And yet I think of him,
looking out at that barn as it always was

from the old house, much the same. With his Eve
who'd never been before so loved it all new.

And then alone. Snow filling the space between.
The same Glenwood stove ticking beside him.

With school out the café's crowded. One family has pushed several tables
together to make one long one. The girl at the counter

tells me her class just painted the 20 on the hill,
a big job, rearranging all the rocks from the 19

and giving them a fresh coat of white. Big job
keeping up with time, as long as you can, while

the metal roof's green oxidizes a softer shade
        and the road bends for the grain silos and straightens

alongside the tracks through thousands of acres of stubble
        and past a parked, red, eight-wheel CASE tractor taller

and no doubt worth more than our old farmhouse ever was.
        But never mind. The point of the Farm was never money,

though Steve puts up a couple hundred round bails
        from neighbors' fields these days, still runs a few Hereford

and keeps up the fences more or less. What my grandpa
        meant for me too with those dying words of his.

And sometimes it's good, staying there, as our nameless woodstove
        warms the damp from inside the cabin

and the whorls and knots map the logs exactly
        as when he used to stop and sit for a visit.

When I gun Elwood for the hill through the woods
        and the rear tires slip a little on wet dirt and pine needles

past the Mossy Rock and the High Centered
        Tractor Stump and the green metal roof comes into view

bowered in aspen between boughs of huge fir,
        there comes a feeling like fear, turning the bolt

and lifting the latch and kicking a tap with the toe of my boot
        to loosen the door I built that always swells tight

against the frame. Always, that anticipation. That emptiness.
    Everything unchanged. His old chair at my desk at the window.

Candles in their holders. Always that stillness. That cold air.
    Amy and I never ran power through the woods up there.

We wanted a deeper seclusion. Anya's bathwater
    warming on the woodstove. The quiet. Antique flicker

in candle and lamplight. And besides, we were all but broke.
    Which explains half the ceiling still insulation backing

where the spendy tongue-and-groove pine ran out.
    And that phone jack just below the steep steps

up to the loft? The line that still runs, long dead now
    underground uphill from where the farmhouse was,

was among the first from the Universal Service Fund
    in '97, just the kind of government program we need more of

everyone on the Farm agreed. The year Anya turned two
    we moved the eighty-six miles to Cheney,

snug up against campus, and let our Idaho number expire.
    But all those others—names and numbers in pencil

and marker and pen—are still on the wall. *Grandma and Grandpa*
    263-6571 in Sharpie among them. "Anya's up

from her nap," we called to say. "Come on up any time."
    Sun on waist-high daisies. Grandma's walking stick.

December of ’67. The phone lines ended at the Evans’.
        Art gets the call, snowshoes the county road

to the mailbox at the end, hollers up
        to the house on the hill, “Roy and Helen!”

They appear in the back door. “You have a grandson!”
        Big reaching waves. It begins. The Amtrak

riverbends through mountains of darkness. Steve
        waits for me in the Sandpoint depot lot. The red pickup’s

exhaust rises in amber lamp atmosphere. Pure Prairie League
        thinking I could stay with her, as I turn

Amy in the cabin kitchen candlelight, fresh batteries
        in the boombox for a while, maybe longer

from the Crown Vic’s six Kenwoods, “Return to the route,” and
        another seltzer from the cooler she packed on the seat beside me.

Everything’s an elegy. Spray of starlings
        from the fenceline, low over the road

and up. The John Deere lifting his ten-bottom plow
        at the pivot, ten clean blades catching sun.

Mud-crusted cattle. Feedlot. Sage and tumbleweed.
        High-volt towers walk their lines to the horizon

day after day after day after day after the yesterday
        that’s dead and gone, and the tomorrow out of sight.

Willie again. Clean and clear as '79. Turquoise
    pickup's wheel in my worn-work-gloved hands.

All I want is back there. And then twenty miles of scrub rangeland
    past Grand Coulee the phone pings Anya's text.

School's stressing her out. Do I have a minute to talk?
    Anya, in washbasin bathwater Amy and I warmed

on the woodstove. Anya, on the far side of the continent
    from me. Down a gravel side road along tumbleweeds

crowding against sagging barbed wire, I park in the sage and get a signal.
    And with the first, distant silhouette glimpse of mountains

under a golden-horizon evening I return to the self
    and love far out beyond where I once belonged.

My daughter's voice. From her dorm in a city.
    My voice to calm her. It's night there.

Dropped phrases. Dropped call. The callback fails.
    I turn Elwood's big engine, turn around. "Return

to the route," and drive faster, glance down to check for signal
    at each long rise until finally her text pings, *I'm doing better,*

thanks! :). Talking helped. Going to try to get some
    more work done. Love you. Not another

person anywhere. No tower to stream my Pandora station.
    Dusk filling the dry creek drainage, borrowed time

of Elwood's cop-motor and cop-tires the only music
for the long downgrade when big cars and old country

have both had their day. About time, the new poets rightly say.
And if Hugo's Buick found its forward-most gear,

it's no less crushed and bailed and shipped off for scrap iron.
That much less the wound we'll make, I know,

with all our latest hunger. But "believe you and I sing tiny and wise,"
I said to gray coffin atop the grave, "and could if we had to

eat stone and go on." And if Grandpa had to die inside
between the chrome rails, what better way than singing

with his sons and grandson, "Oh give me a home"
sweet morphine-smile "happy trails to you"

those blues still blue when we sing from this valley he
is leaving, remember, remember the cowboy

who loved us so true. There's a photo somewhere.
Black and white. I'm six or seven. He's beside me.

Our mud boots and long coats. Farmhouse behind us.
Our shovels. We've been filling the ruts

in the driveway, cutting back the dirt bank to widen the curve.
Looks like a December. No snow yet that year.

No hard freeze. Soon we'll cut a Christmas tree.
Over the bridge at Bridgeport, all that nickel-dull shimmer

of the Columbia with low-gliding raven, I touch the screen.
    Four bars. The buffering wheel turns. Bright, familiar notes.

"Almost heaven" comes and for a change I let it.
    "What is West Virginia?" the Middle Eastern student

shooting hoops on the student family housing court
    with my friends and me asked as he sang,

reminding me of what I considered my home far away.
    I always inserted "northern Idaho"

where the song came with record crackle
    in the little living room, which I could conjure

with the county road gravel sound, forest opening
    to the weathered-from-white farmhouse on the hill,

velvet green timber rising beyond, from my boyhood
    apartment bedroom so far away. And so I drew and drew

that scene, rooflines and windows, fence posts,
    fir and pine and tamarack, and mailbox from memory.

And I wrote. A little like this, in fact, except then
    it was only distance I was trying to cross,

to the place I might belong. That song. Anthem
    of my flannel shirt on the nail. Morning kindling snap

from the Monarch. I heard it once in Scotland, with
    Uncle Steve and Cousin Jennifer, his daughter, raised

on those eighty acres, Grandpa and Grandma's house
        after school, in the White Hart, oldest Inn

in Edinburgh, Graeme E. Pearson nearing the end of his set
        of sing-alongs—"Loch Lomond," "The Skye Boat Song,"

"Dirty Old Town"—and improbably everyone at their loudest
        most vehement for the Mountain Mama! finale,

asking country roads to take us all home. Steve, Jennifer and I
        shouting along, exchanging incredulous smiles, Grandpa

four years beyond our ever going home to tell him.
        And again in Scotland, at the Highland wedding reception

of my other-side cousins Megan and Jon, the Celtic band
        on a break, the dance floor still crowded

for "Islands in the Stream" and "Nine to Five" and Anya
        teaching her cousins the Cotton-Eyed Joe line dance

and then some dance beat and the floor fills all the way in,
        kilts and tartans spinning, cheers and "Almost Heaven!"

A dance version? It's come to this, the song
        Anya proudly told me was written by an alumnus

from her university, homesick for Massachusetts.
        Which has almost as little ring as northern Idaho, so

West Virginia. But home is home, right? Narrow
        Highland roads along loch, over the pass,

and into the glen. The county road now called Beers-Humbird
after the first family farm after you make the turnoff

and the lumber company that skidded that camp kitchen
cut to cut across the valley and left it

for a farmhouse on the hill and sold off the land
in quarter sections and eighties. This stretch

of State Route 17, no doubt, for someone. Home
a ranchstead, out of sight down one of the rare

mailboxed, gravel side roads. For years I didn't listen. Hit *next*
when any John Denver came on, the heart I knew them by

not up for it after Grandpa died and Grandma moved
to Lilac Plaza in Spokane and the house

went cold as the weather. So it's crazy to feel so lonely?
Pasty Cline understands across fifty-eight years

in the darkening interior around me. So it's crazy to think
my love could hold any of them? Driving onto the Farm,

eighty-six miles home from teaching, those few years
we all lived on the place, past the lights in the old house,

and up the steep hay road through the woods to oil-lamp
and candlelight in the cabin window. Stars.

Unbroken darkness across the valley and up Butler Mountain.
Everyone I'd ever loved alive.

It’s almost night on the open, empty range, the sensual
        skin-curve hills. Hawk quill stuck in the dash vent

like an inkwell. The end of Idaho in darkness behind me.
        Moving to be whole again. My Mapquest arrow

pointing beyond confusion. Blue route road and new land
        scrolling down. A freedom. Amy and Anya loving me

all the way into the dusk orchard hills, apple cider air,
        neon red motel clouds, and “Arrived” of Brewster.

Cobweb in Winter

Leaving the car where the barn was,
I followed deer tracks up the snow road.
The cabin door stuck, swollen from the cold.
The fire snapped to life. Out at the woodshed
I split a round of cedar down to a boxful
more kindling. My grandfather did this.
The smell of bark chips and former sunshine
of former summers rose around him as the hatchet
tinked another slender stick of grain from the bolt.
Cold mornings in the farmhouse that's now bare ridge
my grandmother used a small iron handle
to lift a round iron burner from the top
of the Monarch and feed in the crumpled
Daily Bee and a few sticks of his cedar.
When they could afford it and sometimes anyway
they'd head south for the winter to sit outside.
It's good to think of them there now
forty years ago. She left a paper cup
atop the pickup's column shifter to remind him
to turn off the headlights after they'd pulled
into the apartment parking lot, back from a park.
I write all this but it's still gone. They're gone.
There's a stand of birch at the edge of forest
across the alfalfa field from here.
On his walks around the home place he'd stop,
find his wax pencil in a branch crook,
and write on the bark the date and a few words.
6/12/79 SUNSHINE JON CHOSE CABIN SITE
When I last searched that grove for his lines
they were finally gone, all but a letter
or number here and there on one standing dead

that stopped peeling off its strips of parchment.
And one remaining word in his hand. *YUMA*
Were they just back? All packed to go?
Soon enough, maybe I'll be an old man.
Meanwhile, fir boughs hang out the window.
The same mountain keeps rising to disappear
into a low ceiling of January clouds.

Hypochondria Coping Strategy with Barn

The door stands open
—Epictetus

If you have to kill something you go out to the barn,
which is what he did, the neighbor above our cabin,
called the county sheriff to stop by later,
walked out with the rifle and only himself.
Everywhere I've been, the smell of barn's the same,
an air up from the earth, like the wood and hay,
temporarily, dry manure in summer. Small light
fills the largeness, sun shafts in by day between shakes and boards
that wall and ceiling back solid at night around a hanging bulb.
When the fright comes relentless over me, pins my mind
inside its little, sorry hovel of Maybe, or Incurability,
I take slim comfort in a line, traced straight between temples,
right to left, the rehearsal of an end to end ending's contemplation.
The shortest distance. When I was ten I knew
the exact and singular joy of pouring raw milk on my Wheaties
from the wide-mouth jars our neighbor sold it in,
the creamy sweetness and thick, sweet crunch of each sharp flake.
His diagnosis was years away. His bullet.
Who thought then of dying, really? Someone, but not me.

Unstacking the Wood

The two rows of split and seasoned left
at the back of the cabin's woodshed
have to come out so the fresh-split green
can go back there for next year.
The dry lengths for this coming winter
are light when I pull and send them arcing
over the pile of new to clunk
in a second pile farther out there.
Doubtless, there was a better way to do this.
A plan. Bisect the shed into bays?
Build an entire second shed and rotate?
But if I'm a joke I can't work out
the punch line. At the least I suppose
I could have tossed all this out
before cutting, hauling, and splitting the more
that now blocks much of the way in or out.
I am not irked or impatient with myself.
Smell all that fir and larch? I was mostly
just happy in each moment. Alive.

Whose Name was writ in Water

Maybe let the mountain
creek, cool on my feet
as I lay on the bank
looking where the spruce
point, the creek whose
syllable never ceases, pianissimo
under snow, forte in spring,
companionable now it's July,
the creek whose meaning
is only itself, voice
following its open course
through forest—this creek,
maybe let it do the speaking.
I've come far again
to the long exhale for clouds.
To blood slowing through
vessels of my neck.
Of my sore hands. Soft. Soft.
Soft. I've come to quiet
the alarm of my ears. Hello stone
summits. Hello last of last
winter's high snowfields.
Hello mossy smell rising
in dry alpine air. Hello spires
of grass rising around my face.
Maybe let the creek be the poem.
Somewhere last night's wolf,
alone in this narrow valley,
lowers her pink tongue to drink.

Valley of the Present Perfect

When I returned after many years
my easeful happiness changed nothing.
Through thousands of darknesses the river
had moved without a name.
The mountain's forest bristle had pulled
strands from low-passing clouds.
Every light that came to the long curve of grass
had come without my affection. Every rain,
jeweled on leaves of wild rose
in morning sun. And in ten thousand nights
and days, the valley will have been itself,
snow, crane song, elk bones, lightning, still air
of another last, lingering sunlight without me.

the holiness of the Heart's affections

First comes the trumpet
through a slender neck
beyond sight then flying
over the pair of geese
are briefly embodied
low autumn sun silvers
with every downstroke
the underside of one's wing
as they trade *oie* for *oie*
I who cannot call myself
a believer call up to them
loud enough that they
might hear Good Morning!
softer Godspeed as they pass
back into the everything
unseen beyond the pines

Among Riverbank Cottonwoods

—late afternoon sun, Northern Rockies

This morning's wolves on the far bank are gone.
The valley opens every direction from here,
sage field to far slopes of timber.
On my back in the grass I hear three categories of sound—
wind through high cottonwood leaves and low willow fronds,
the river over boulders, and far and near birdsong.
To shade my face so I may study the blue sky,
I stand this journal upright on my chest.
The tiny fibers along the top of the rough-cut page
glow golden like a ridgeline of grass in the set sun.
My fleece is balled for a pillow beneath my head.
Breeze flows through the hair on my arms.
There are no clouds to follow for thought.
From a high branch across my vision, a swallow.
Three hundred, ninety-one days, the friend
who knew me best has been dead.
I am here. Alive and happy in this field
where many beings have died.

Amy

This morning I heard wolves through mountain rain.
In thin, first light the low sky wet my face.
The subject was loneliness. Always, again, loneliness.
We are each our own piece of this world a while.
From my body across the valley I watched
them find one another, four, and sniff and wag
and turn circles of joy and trot off together.
I drove three hours of mountain road to call you.